Every Child a Song

Nicola Davies

Illustrated by
Marc Martin

Crocodile Books, USA
An imprint of Interlink Publishing Group, Inc.
www.interlinkbooks.com

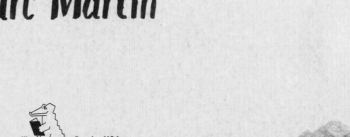

Foreword
by Nicola Davies

The United Nations is a club that almost all the countries of the world belong to. Representatives from those countries meet at the United Nations headquarters in New York City, USA, to talk about big problems, like war and hunger, and to try to find solutions that make the world better for everyone.

A very important part of the UN's work is to improve the lives of children all over the Earth. To help with this, the UN made a list of the things that every child needs to be healthy and happy and to grow up into a good citizen of the world. It's called the UN Convention on the Rights of the Child (the UNCRC for short), because every child in the world has a right to get what they need.

That doesn't mean the right to "candy every day" or "all the toys I want!" It means things like the right to be cared for by your family or by other grown-ups who do the best for you, and the right to an education that helps you become the best you can be, no matter who you are and where you come from.

Unfortunately, there are many millions of children all over the world who are not protected from harm, war, or hunger, who have no grown-ups to care for them, and who can't get an education. The UNCRC is important because it speaks up for those children. It says to the world that their suffering is wrong and that, together, we must do better, so that every child can grow up with a song in their heart.

When you were born, a song began.

Sometimes it didn't sound much like a song.
Sometimes, no one could hear it.

But it was there in every heartbeat,
every breath; tiny, fragile, and unique.

A melody the world had never heard before.

It needed love to help it grow,
to keep it sheltered and protected.
Nourished, cherished, celebrated.

It needed naming and belonging,
a home to call its own,
arms to hold it safe in warmth and welcome.

Then with each new step and word,
your song picked up its rhythm.

It soared...explored!

It learned the blue of sky,
the green of leaves,
the red of dawn and sunset.

All around you, everywhere,
other songs are singing.

Some are loud,
and some are quiet,

some sing a single note
and some a symphony.

Whatever melody a song sings,
each one is true and beautiful;
unique and special as your own.

No song should be worn away to silence ...

No song should be drowned out...

nor stolen, and made to sing
the tune of darkness,
hate,
or war.

Even among storm and change and danger,
every song must be heard above the noise
and chaos of the world.

Because when every child is born, a song begins...

a melody the world has never heard before.
Unique and tiny.
Fragile.
But never quite alone.

For together, we raise our voices

for the right of every song to sing out loud, bold and unafraid.

So, small new song, sing on, lifelong.
Sing love, sing joy, sing freedom!

The Rights of the UNCRC

There are 54 rights listed in the UNCRC, and they're known as the 54 articles. That's too many to write about in one picture book, but here are some of the rights that I thought about most as I was writing:

Article 6 | Life, survival, and development
Every child has the right to life. Governments must do all they can to ensure that children survive and develop to their full potential.

Article 13 | Freedom of expression
Every child must be free to express their thoughts and opinions.

Article 14 | Freedom of thought, belief, and religion
Every child has the right to think and believe what they choose.

Article 15 | Freedom of association
Every child has the right to meet with other children and to join groups and organizations, as long as this does not stop other people from enjoying their rights.

Article 19 | Protection from violence, abuse, and neglect
Governments must do all they can to ensure that children are protected from all forms of violence, abuse, neglect, and bad treatment by their parents or anyone else who looks after them.

Article 22 | Refugee children
If a child is seeking refuge or has refugee status, governments must provide them with protection and assistance. Governments must help refugee children who are separated from their parents to be reunited with them.

Article 23 | Children with a disability

A child with a disability has the right to live a full life with dignity and, as far as possible, independence. Governments must do all they can to support disabled children.

Article 28 | Right to education

Every child has the right to an education.

Article 31 | Leisure, play, and culture

Every child has the right to relax, play, and take part in a wide range of cultural and artistic activities.

Article 32 | Child labor

Governments must protect children from work that is dangerous or that might harm their health, development, or education. Governments must set a minimum age for children to work.

I also thought about the last few rights in the Convention, articles 43 to 54. They aren't listed here, but they are very important. They say that adults and governments should do all they can to make sure that children around the world get the rights laid out in the UNCRC.

In 2020 it will be thirty years since the UNCRC came into effect, so I wrote this book to say "Happy Birthday," and to celebrate what the Convention can do for children. Perhaps by the time the UNCRC reaches its sixtieth birthday, every child will grow up enjoying all the rights for which it stands.

For children who are alone.
With love – N.D.

First published in the USA in 2020 by

Crocodile Books
An imprint of Interlink Publishing Group, Inc.
46 Crosby Street, Northampton, MA 01060
www.interlinkbooks.com

Published simultaneously in the UK by Wren & Rook, an Imprint of Hachette Children's Group

Articles of the UNCRC adapted from:
https://downloads.unicef.org.uk/wp-content/uploads/2010/05/UNCRC_summary-1.pdf?_
ga=2.57215594.1189250842.1548673288-1833875586.1546433030

Library of Congress Cataloging-in-Publication Data available
ISBN 978-1-62371-872-5

10 9 8 7 6 5 4 3 2 1

Printed and bound in China

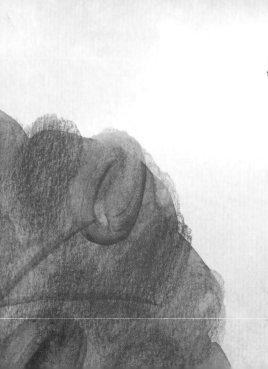